DINOSAURS
AND PREHISTORIC
ANIMALS

Written by Jack Long
Photography by Ardea London
Arthur Hayward
with Peter Green and Pat Morris
Illustrations by Wilcock: Riley Graphic Art Limited

Introduction

Tyrannosaurus Rex: One of the Largest Dinosaurs

Tyrannosaurus Rex (tye-ran-O-SAWR-us) has often been called the king of the dinosaurs. Most dinosaur scholars believe that Tyrannosaurus was one of the largest flesh-eating animals that ever lived on land. This giant was 16 to 20 feet high. Standing next to Tyrannosaurus Rex, a person would have only reached its knee, but there were no people on Earth when it was alive from 100 million to 70 million years ago.

There were, however, many other dinosaurs. All of them feared the mighty hunter, Tyrannosaurus Rex. From its huge mouth, with daggerlike teeth, to the tip of its tail, it was 50 feet long. Its short upper limbs were clawed, as were its powerful hind feet.

It seemed to be the ruler of its world as it roamed over what today is North America, bringing terror to smaller dinosaurs. Yet it vanished from Earth, while other dinosaurs lived on for many more years. What happened? Why did it fail to survive? And why did all of the dinosaurs disappear from Earth?

Scientists have clues and theories that you will discover in the pages that follow.

Tyrannosaurus Rex

Compsognathus

Compsognathus:
The Smallest of the Dinosaurs

Compsognathus (COMP-sog-NATE-us), that lived 150 million years ago, was no bigger than a chicken. This smallest of dinosaurs was no more than 2 feet tall and walked, or maybe hopped, on long, delicate legs.

The best fossil skeleton print of Compsognathus was found in limestone deposits in Germany. From this print, scientists have figured that it walked in an erect position and lived on shores of shallow lakes. Its favorite foods were small reptiles (such as lizards and turtles) and insects. In this small lagoon world, Compsognathus was king. But in the world away from the lake shore there were larger animals that considered it a tasty morsel. Fortunately, it was a fast runner and could dart away quickly from its giant enemies to hide among the early trees and ferns then growing on earth.

The fossil skull of Compsognathus shows that it had sharp, little teeth, which is proof that it was a flesh eater, or as scientists would say, a carnivore. The head of Compsognathus was about 3 inches long and it was perched on a long, slender neck. Its tail, as you can see from the picture, was much longer than its head, neck, and body all together.

Like the huge Tyrannosaurus Rex, Compsognathus lived in a pleasant world with a warm climate and with plenty of food available. Yet it vanished with the rest of the dinosaurs. Compsognathus, too, is a part of the puzzle of why dinosaurs disappeared from Earth.

7

The Coming of the Dinosaurs

Before the dinosaurs appeared on Earth many, many things had happened. At first, nearly 5,000 million years ago, our globe was made up of molten rock—rock so hot it had melted. Heavy clouds of steam swirled about Earth. It took millions of years for Earth to cool, but when it did, the rains came. Seas and lakes were formed and very small plants, called algae, began growing in the water.

The Paleozoic Era:

Much, much later the first animals appeared. By 500 million years ago the seas were home for tiny animals, such as coral, jellyfish, and trilobites. Scientists have named this the Paleozoic Era. In this age, about 440 million years ago, the first fish swam the seas and plants began to grow on the land. Then around 300 million years ago, the earliest reptiles are known to have existed.

The Strange Reptiles:

Among the first amphibians, animals that lived both on land and in the water, was Eryops. Almost all of its life was spent near or in the water. This time was known as the Age of Amphibians. Scientists also refer to this time as the Carboneferous Period. Most of the coal from Earth comes from the great forests at that time. There were giant trees and plants growing in the swamps. As they fell into the swamps, they became fossilized. After millions of years, they turned into coal. As mentioned, plants and trees now grew everywhere, and in the steamy jungles there were huge dragonflies, such as Meganeura. The Meganeura had wings that measured over 2 feet from tip to tip. Spiders, scorpions, grasshoppers, and cockroaches scurried about. Millions of years had passed, and now the planet was teeming with life, although the Age of the Dinosaurs was far away in the future.

The Age of Amphibians:

In time the reptiles appeared on land. Closely related to the amphibians, reptiles are cold-blooded animals that have an outer covering of scales (like snakes) or horny plates (like turtles). They found living on land much easier. For one thing, the eggs they laid had thick, hard shells and there was little chance that the amphibian babies inside the shell would dry up as sometimes happened with the thin-shelled amphibian eggs.

One of these new reptiles that developed has been named Dimetrodon (dye-MET-ro-don). It lived about 265 million years ago and was a carnivore, or flesh eater, with sharp teeth. It grew 6 to 10 feet in length. Its "sail" (the spiny ridge on its back) rose up 2 or 3 feet above its backbone. Dimetrodon was a cold-blooded animal. Scientists think its "sail" may have been filled with blood vessels, which quickly heated up in the morning sun. When it became hot, it turned away from the sun to cool off. Thus it adapted well to the extremes of heat and cold on the desert, where it often lived in what is now the southwest United States. Dimetrodon was the ruler of its small world, since it was one of the largest and one of the most active animals living.

The Stem Reptiles:

The earliest reptiles, like Dimetrodon, were called cotylosaurs, or "stem reptiles." The family of cotylosaurs, which was large, developed through the years in different ways. One kind became a species from which turtles evolved. Another kind became the ancestors of the dinosaurs.

Meganeura

Dimetrodon

The Early Dinosaurs

Dinosaurs lived during the Mesozoic Era. This is known as the "middle life" of Earth. The earliest dinosaurs are believed to have appeared during the first part of the Mesozoic Era, which is called the Triassic Period. Triassic comes from the Latin word meaning three. Three rock layers were formed during the Triassic Period. The time span for the period was about 35 million years, or from 225 to 190 million years ago.

Euparkeria

Enter the Euparkeria:

The word dinosaur means "terrible lizard," although dinosaurs are not lizards. Euparkeria (yoo-park-ER-e-ya) was not very terrible and was certainly rather small by dinosaur standards. It was about 3 feet long and lived in Africa some 200 million years ago. Euparkeria probably walked on all four feet, but when it was in a hurry, it got up on its strong hind legs and ran. It was able to stand because its legs were directly beneath its body, not spread out on each side like a reptile's legs.

There were two major dinosaur families. One family was known as Saurischian, which means lizard-like. The other family is called Ornithischian, or bird-like. These terms apply to the differences in their hip bones. All Saurischian dinosaurs have hip bones that work much like a lizard's. Ornithischian, on the other hand, had hips shaped like those of a bird. All the bird-hipped dinosaurs were plant eaters. Most of the Saurischian were flesh eaters. Euparkeria belonged to the Saurischian family.

After Euparkeria came many, many other dinosaurs, which we shall meet in the following pages. For about 150 million years these creatures were the rulers of Earth.

Meanwhile in North America:

At the same time that Euparkeria lived in Africa, an early ancestor of the dinosaur lived in North America. Its name was Rutiodon (ROO-ti-o-don) and it resembled a crocodile. Supposedly, Rutiodon first fed on plants. The name comes from the Greek "rhytes," which is the word for plant, and "odon," which is the word for tooth.

hip bones of Saurischian dinosaur

hip bones of Ornithischian dinosaur

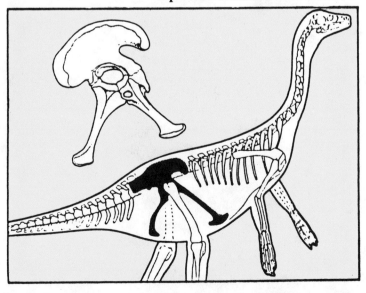

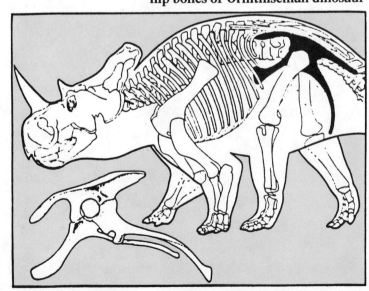

Stegosaurus (left) and Ceratosaurus (right) fighting

An Unequal Fight

The picture shows a fight between a Stegosaurus (STEG-uh-SAWR-us) and a Ceratosaurus (seh-RAT-uh-SAWR-us). Stegosaurus is the one with a double row of bony plates from the back of its neck to the tip of its tail. Notice the sharp, daggerlike teeth of Ceratosaurus. It is a flesh-eating dinosaur.

Stegosaurus was a plant-eating dinosaur. Its name means "roofed lizard" because the first scholars that studied it thought the hollow, horny plates looked somewhat like roof shingles. However, at first it was thought that the plates *were* made of solid bone. Now there is evidence that they were not hollow but were filled with blood vessels, like the dinosaur Dimetrodon.

Why is the fight unequal? Ceratosaurus was a much larger dinosaur. It often reached 40 feet in length and weighed as much as 6 tons. Stegosaurus was only from 18 to 20 feet in length and weighed 2 to 3 tons. The best defense that Stegosaurus had was its spiked tail; yet, as you can see in the picture, it

was unable to use it. Moreover, most scientists agree that Stegosaurus was not very smart and was easily confused. Its brain was quite small, possibly no larger than a walnut.

Where is the fight happening? Both dinosaurs roamed the countryside of what is now western and northwestern United States. Their fossil remains have been found in Colorado and Wyoming.

Wherever the plant eaters, such as Stegosaurus, went to find food, the flesh-eating Ceratosaurus followed to prey on the more peaceful plant eaters. Ceratosaurus also had savage talons on its four feet that served as sharp weapons.

Both dinosaurs lived from 160 million to 135 million years ago. They, too, disappeared with the rest of the dinosaurs. The warring flesh eaters must have been partly to blame for the increasingly small number of plant eaters. As their food supply dwindled, the flesh eaters also may have been in trouble. To live one had to have something to eat.

Plesiosaur bones

The Plesiosaur, Reptile of the Sea:

Fossils were eventually discovered that belonged to reptiles that ruled the seas. These dinosaurs of the sea lived at the same time as the dinosaurs which lived on the land. Some of these sea dinosaurs had ancestors who once lived on land. Over millions of years they returned to the water, finding they could live there more successfully.

The name Plesiosaur (plees-i-o-SAWR) means "near lizard." This was a dinosaur that spent its life in the sea. Here it paddled along the surface of the sea or just beneath it. Its long neck twisted and turned quickly to catch its diet of fish. Indeed, its mouth, with long, sharp, closely spaced teeth, was a fish trap that easily held on to the slippery fish.

The Plesiosaur abounded in the waters of the Mesozoic Era, or middle life, of Earth. It was a large creature and known to have lived in the Jurassic seas. Some Plesiosaurs reached a length of almost 40 feet.

In northern Scotland there is a lake called Loch Ness, where many people have claimed to see a long-necked monster swimming. It has been suggested that it might be a surviving member of the Plesiosaur family.

How the Plesiosaur Lived:

It is known that the Plesiosaur had to come to the surface of the sea for air. Some scholars think that, like turtles, it pulled itself up on the beach to lay its eggs and then buried them in the warm sand. It did not stay around to wait for the eggs to hatch. When the baby Plesiosaurs broke out of their eggs, they had to make their way to the water by themselves. The journey was short but it was also very dangerous. Sometimes there were hungry enemies waiting to pounce. The baby Plesiosaurs could easily be eaten by land crabs or flying reptiles or any carnivorous creature.

The Plesiosaurs were among the most successful dinosaurs, in terms of survival. They lasted through the Age of Dinosaurs. Then they, too, vanished from the seas. Some people who have studied dinosaurs think there was a cooling period on Earth. The warm seas that were filled with so much life became too cold for many of the creatures to live. With the food supply at low ebb, many Plesiosaurs may not have had enough to eat in order to stay alive, or perhaps the sand in which the eggs were buried became too cool to hatch the baby Plesiosaurs.

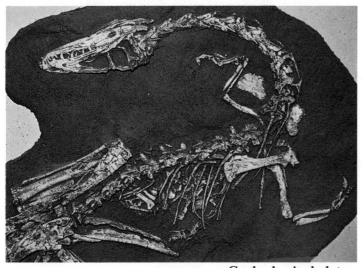
Coelophysis skeleton

Diplodocus

A Jigsaw Puzzle

Deciding how a dinosaur looked is not easy. Remember, no human has ever seen a dinosaur. We can only imagine how they looked. Like detectives, scholars work with many clues. A fossil footprint, a few scattered bones, the shape of a dinosaur tooth are some of the clues. Footprints can tell how the dinosaur walked. Sometimes enough bones are found for scientists to imagine how the other bones were shaped. Then they reconstruct an entire skeleton.

From the Coelophysis (see-o-LO-fiz-is) skeleton pictured on this page, scholars figured out that this dinosaur must have been about 8 feet long and that it walked on two legs. It had saw-like teeth and probably ate anything that was smaller than it was.

The giant Diplodocus (dip-lo-DOK-us) was probably 88 feet long. Sometimes a piece of skin is found still covering bones, much like an Egyptian mummy.

From the bones of Brachiosaurus (BRAK-e-o-SAWR-us), it was determined that this was one of the largest of all dinosaurs. No other bones as large as those of Brachiosaurus have been found. Standing over 40 feet tall, it could easily have looked over the top of a house, had there been any houses at that time.

Footprints indicate that it could gallop as fast as 15 miles per hour. A herd of Brachiosaurus racing across the plains would almost have made the ground shake.

Size comparison of Brachiosaurus and modern horse

The Giants

Brontosaurus, The Thunder Lizard:

Among the largest dinosaurs was Brontosaurus (BRONT-o-SAWR-us). The name means "thunder lizard" and it is easy to guess that these giants, that traveled in herds, would have made a sound like thunder as they pounded across the meadows and marshes. They lived in North America and Europe between 120 and 155 million years ago. It has been estimated that one Brontosaurus weighed as much as six elephants. Yet this dinosaur could probably travel as quickly as an elephant. Its head, however, was not at all like an elephant's. Brontosaurus' head was not any thicker than its long neck. Even so, it was able to swallow a half-a-ton of food each day.

The Brontosaurus must have spent all their waking hours eating or searching for food. They were plant eaters and needed enormous amounts of food to satisfy their hunger. They mostly lived in marshes or on the banks of streams where food was easier to find.

Allosaurus, Or "Other Lizard:"

Allosaurus means "other lizard." It was much fiercer than the plant-eating Brontosaurus. Allosaurus was one of the largest flesh-eating dinosaurs of its time. A mighty hunter with huge teeth that were 3 inches long, curved claws on its feet, Allosaurus lived in western North America about 150 million years ago. Standing upright, Allosaurus could measure 30 feet long. With its great head and clawed feet, Allosaurus must have been terrifying.

As previously mentioned, scientists can only speculate as to how dinosaurs really lived. New evidence always arises. Until recently it was believed that Allosaurus fed only on dinosaurs that were already dead. Later clues have convinced most scientists that Allosaurus often killed its victims. No one is sure whether Allosaurus hunted alone or in a pack. Because of its strength and fierceness it could easily have killed plant-eating dinosaurs that were at least two or three times its size.

Allosaurus

Stegosaurus, The Armored Lizard:

On page 11 of this book you can see an attack on Stegosaurus, the plant-eating dinosaur, by Ceratosaurus, the fiercer flesh-eating dinosaur.

Stegosaurus was a slow, rather peaceful dinosaur, in comparison to most of the other dinosaurs you have so far read about. Rather than risking a vicious fight, this dinosaur would often run for cover.

The armored double row of plates along the back of Stegosaurus have caused scientists to refer to it as a "cover lizard." An interesting feature of Stegosaurus is that, in effect, it had two brains. One brain was a tiny one in its head. Twenty times larger was a "brain" which was actually an enlargement of its spinal cord at its hip. Scientists believe that this "brain" controlled the movement of its heavy hind legs and its powerful tail, with which the dinosaur defended itself.

Its fore limbs were much shorter than its hind limbs, which made it easy for the Stegosaurus to search for the plants it loved to eat. But this fact made it more difficult to watch for enemies. Possibly this is why it disappeared earlier than some of the other dinosaurs.

Stegosaurus

Pteranodon

Pteranodon, A Living Glider:

The giant flying reptiles that ruled the skies 120 million to 60 million years ago belonged to a family named Pterosaur, meaning "winged lizard."

This bat-like creature had a membrane that stretched from the tip of its claw, down to its leg. Pterosaurs were initially believed to be cold-blooded. Recently, however, one was discovered in the Soviet Union with the remains of hair on its body. The hair tells us that this creature was warm-blooded.

The largest member of the Pterosaur family was the Pteranodon (ter-AN-o-don), which means "toothless wing." Its wingspan was usually 22 to 26 feet, although a very large Pteranodon whose fossil remains were found in Texas had a wingspan of 50 feet.

Pteranodon was a fierce hunter. It had a big beak and a long, bony horn on the back of its head. For a reptile, it had a large brain and keen sight.

Pteranodon glided or soared. It needed steady, gentle winds in which to fly. When the climate was warm these winds were present, but when Earth had a long cooling period, the winds became much rougher. Scientists think the Pteranodon could not battle these high winds and could no longer glide about in search of food. That was probably what caused the end of Pteranodon.

Crested Hadrosaur

Crested Hadrosaur, A Duck-Billed Dinosaur:

There were many kinds of Hadrosaurs (had-ro-SAWR), but generally they were not very different, except for the shapes of their heads. Eighty million years ago, Hadrosaur was one of the most common dinosaurs in North America. Scientists know a lot about the Hadrosaur because fossilized mummies have been found complete with the skin still covering the bones. One was found in Kansas in 1908. The one you see here was called a Parasaurolophus (PAR-a-sawr-o-LOAS-us). It was an excellent swimmer. Being particularly fond of water plants, it spent most of its time in and around water.

An interesting feature of Parasaurolophus was the crest growing from the back of its head. It was hollow, and scientists think it was a sort of extra nose. When Parasaurolophus swam under water, looking for food, the "extra" nose may have served as an air-storage chamber. Possibly the Parasaurolophus had a stronger sense of smell because of its crest (or, "extra" nose).

Another interesting feature was that it was always growing new teeth. In its lifetime it often produced as many as 2,000!

Although Hadrosaur was large, from 33 to 40 feet long, it was a mild, peaceful creature. It had no means of defense against its enemies, mainly the flesh-eating dinosaurs, except that it was a speedy swimmer. With its keen sense of smell, it could detect an approaching enemy and swim quickly into deeper water. With its webbed feet, which were excellent paddles, it could outdistance many of the other dinosaurs that were slow, rather clumsy swimmers. Size and speed, however, were not enough. In the end, Hadrosaur did not outlast its many dinosaur enemies.

Iguanodon, The First Dinosaur Discovered:

In 1822 in England, the wife of Dr. Gideon Mantell made a strange discovery. She was out walking when she came upon a large tooth sticking from a rock. She took it home to her husband, who was a scientist. At this time no one had ever heard of dinosaurs. The term did not even exist. Dr. Mantell showed the tooth to other scientists and, after much research, it was decided that the tooth resembled the present day iguana's, although it was much larger. So they named the animal belonging to the tooth Iguanodon (i-GWAN-o-don). Then in 1877 a group of miners digging in a tunnel in Belgium found the complete skeletons of 23 Iguanodons. Because of this discovery we know a great deal about this dinosaur. We know that Iguanodons travelled in herds, probably as a way to protect and defend themselves. It is now believed, based on this evidence and other findings much like this, that many of the plant-eating dinosaurs were herd-living creatures.

Iguanodon lived over 100 million years ago in Europe and North Africa. It was a plant eater. Its average height was about 16 feet and its length 30 feet. It weighed nearly seven tons. Practically its only means of defending itself were its sharp, daggerlike thumbs.

Iguanodon was an elephant-sized dinosaur. It could crouch down to eat plants or stand up to nibble on tree branches. Although it looked dangerous, it was no match for the fast and fierce flesh-eating dinosaurs.

Iguanodon

Triceratops

Triceratops, The Last of the Horned Dinosaurs:

Triceratops (try-SER-a-tops) means three-horned face. Its enormous head, which was 7 feet long, had a stout horn on its nose and two other horns, one over each eye. The horns were not just for show. Although Triceratops was a plant-eating dinosaur, it was also a fighter. It fought other Triceratops as well as any enemy that might attack it. Chief enemy of Triceratops was Tyrannosaurus Rex that lived in the same place (North America) and at the same time (some 70 million years ago). Although Tyrannosaurus Rex was twice as large, it probably hesitated to attack Triceratops unless it was very hungry. Twenty to 30 feet long and weighing up to 10 tons, Triceratops could charge like an army tank.

Along with all the rest of the dinosaurs, Triceratops disappeared from Earth. Most scientists think a climate change from warm weather, which produced many plants and made living easy for the dinosaur, to a colder, harsher climate, was the chief cause. All that is known for sure is that some disaster that happened on Earth about 65 million years ago destroyed all the great dinosaurs.

It makes our life more interesting to learn about dinosaurs through the studies of thoughtful scientists who have been able to show us how these giant creatures lived. What an exciting place Earth must have been during the Age of the Dinosaurs. What a safer place it is for us now that they no longer roam the land!